NATIONAL GEOGRAPHIC KiDS

weird but true!

COOL and CRAZY STICKER DOODLE BOOK

THAT'S WEIRD!

This book belongs to:
Brooklynn Olinger

NATIONAL GEOGRAPHIC KiDS

weird but true!

COOL and CRAZY STICKER DOODLE BOOK

KELLY HARGRAVE

NATIONAL GEOGRAPHIC
WASHINGTON, D.C.

COOL

WONDERFUL

RY YEAR FINLAND HOSTS THE AIR GUITAR WORLD CHAMPIONSHIPS. • A SUIT OF ARMOR M
SE MORE THAN 8,000 POUNDS (3,629 KG) OF CANDY HELD IN A SIX-STORY PIÑATA. • PAC-M
IONAL ICE CREAM FOR BREAKFAST DAY. • SCIENTISTS FOUND A 99-MILLION-YEAR-OLD DI
... HAS A SCULPTURE OF DARTH VADER'S HEAD ON IT. • ONE ASTRONAUT TOOK DIRT FROM
SEUM IN A FREIGHT ELEVATOR. IT ALLOWS ONLY THREE PEOPLE IN AT A TIME! • A SHIPPIN
E SINCE BEEN FOUND ALL OVER THE WORLD—IN HAWAII, U.S.A.; AUSTRALIA; AND EVEN
FIRST WHALES HAD LEGS. • THE ANNUAL TOMATO THROWING FESTIVAL IN SPAIN HOLDS
E WITH FIVE ROUNDS OF BOXING. • THE ORIGINAL MR. POTATO HEAD TOY USED A REAL PO
L SOMEONE WHERE TO DIG FOR TREASURE. • A MOUSE CAN FIT THROUGH A HOLE THE SIZE
CODILES SOMETIMES CLIMB TREES. • PAINTING WAS ONCE AN OLYMPIC SPORT. • PLAY-DO
TAIN SHARKS WALK ON THEIR FINS UNDERWATER. • A FIRE STARTED BY SCIENTISTS MOR
SSES FOR INSECTS. • DRAGON-BOAT RACERS CAN ROW THE LENGTH OF 4.5 FOOTBALL FIEL
HICKEN RESTAURANT ONCE GAVE AWAY PHONE CASES SHAPED LIKE GIANT DRUMSTICKS.
R OWN SUBMARINE. • A LEGO SCULPTURE OF ENGLAND'S QUEEN ELIZABETH II INCLUDED
EGRINE FALCONS CAN DIVE 15 TIMES FASTER THAN THE OCEAN'S FASTEST DIVER, THE
ENTISTS FOUND SHARKS LIVING IN AN UNDERWATER VOLCANO. • A COMPANY IN ENGLAND
E PLANT GROWS ONLY ON TOP OF DIAMOND DEPOSITS. • T. REX'S ARMS WERE SO SHORT,
ICING TO MUSIC AS THE STORE'S SIGNAL. • SOME WORMS THAT LIVE ON CORAL REEFS LOOK L
R DOWN A 100-FOOT (30-M) SLIDE AT 50 MILES AN HOUR (80 KM/H). • WATER POLO PLAYE
W WITHOUT ANY CLOUDS IN THE SKY. • ACCORDING TO ONE STUDY, SURGEONS WHO PLAY V
ALLY BE CONSIDERED A PICKLE UNLESS IT BOUNCES. • IN THE FUTURE, YOU MAY BE ABLE
GOLD IN EARTH'S CRUST. • THERE ARE FIVE TIMES AS MANY BICYCLES AS CARS IN COPEN
ERSON WHO IS LEARNING THE ALPHABET. • SOME DIAMONDS FALL TO EARTH FROM OUTER
E BALLS AT ONCE. • THERE IS A VARIETY OF LEMON CALLED A BABOON. • SCIENTISTS THIN
CIENT GAS CLOUD. • BACTERIA TALK TO EACH OTHER. • SOME SCIENTISTS THINK THAT PLA
GIN. • DANCING BEARS. • FIREFLIES CAN GLOW YELLOW, GREEN, OR ORANGE. • A
LD BE A HALF A MILE (0.8 KM) LONG. • A DONUT TOPPED WITH SPRINKL
ING ONLINE. • PIGS TEND TO SLEEP IN A FULL
EOPLE ON EARTH IS STRONG ENO
NIP TEA TO FELINE GUESTS. • IN CALIFORNIA, U.S.A., YOU CAN
G BARK PARK INN IN IDAHO, U.S.A. • COLLEG
R VEGETABLES. • BEFORE CANDY WAS CALLED "
MOYA FRUIT, NATIVE TO SOUTH AMERICA, TASTES LIKE BBLE
BBLE THAT WAS LARGER THAN A BASKETBALL. • YOU FORGET MOST OF YOUR
ITS MOUTH. **• DOODLING CAN HELP YOU CONCENTRATE. •** ELECTRIC EELS CA
TYPUSES CAN FEEL THE ELECTRIC FIELDS PUT OUT BY OTHER ANIMALS. •
TO DOLLS AND ACTION FIGURES. YOUR FINGERNAILS GROW AT LEAS
HE SUMMER. SOME BUTTERFLIES' EARS ARE ON THEIR WINGS. BUTTERFLIES LIV
A WRESTLING MATCH IN 12 GALLONS OF GRAVY. • A HIGH HEEL RACE =
ING RACE = BABIES CRAWL 12 FEET (3.7 ... FISH LIKE. • ROACH RACIN
T NEW YORK CITY'S BRONX ZOO, YOU CAN ... CAROUSEL ON GIANT INSECT
S.A. • THE NATIONAL ZOO IN WASHINGTON, D.C., U.S.A., HAS A SOLAR-POWERE
HATS. • A TOILET-SHAPED MOTORBIKE IN TOKYO USES FUEL MADE FROM ANIM

4

How to Use This Book

Welcome to the wacky world of **Weird But True!** You've stumbled upon the most outrageous activity book in existence, full of bizarre facts you might not believe are actually real. And as you ponder exciting info about the strangeness of space, **outlandish legends**, astounding animals, surprising sports, and much more, you might find yourself saying things like, "That's unbelievable!" or "What?! That's RIDICULOUS!" They are all so very weird!

So prepare to take every mind-blowing fact to the next level, with prompts to doodle and draw, solve playful puzzles, decode mysterious messages, race through mazes, search for odd objects, and **unscramble the unpredictable!**

Don't forget to decorate your genius creations with the **150 cool and crazy stickers** included in this book. And if a puzzle has you stumped, have no fear! The answers are in the back of the book.

So stretch out those doodling hands and grab a pencil or a pen, a bucketful of crayons, markers, colored pencils, or all of the above, and get ready to turn the page and ignite your incredible imagination. **3 ... 2 ... 1 ... GO!**

Every year Finland hosts the AIR GUITAR World Championships.

Draw outrageous instruments for each of these awesome air guitarists. Give the guitars different shapes or cool patterns—one of the guitarists could even be air banjoing!

Fireflies can glow yellow, green, or orange.

Connect the fireflies to see what glowing shape they make.

In New York City
there is a tiny museum in
a **freight elevator.**
It allows only **three people**
in at a time!

A
SUIT of **ARMOR**
made for a
GUINEA PIG
sold for **$24,000**
more than online.

Now that their guinea pig pal has protection, these other animals want in! Finish decking out these creatures with the most daring defenses you can dream up. Like real medieval knights, give each animal a special symbol on their shield.

8

The Titanic
holicaust
history

If you could create your own museum, what would it focus on? Fill this museum room with artifacts that you think are museum worthy.

Ring
Piggy

An abecedarian is a person who is learning the alphabet.

For each letter of the alphabet, write your favorite word or the funniest word that comes to mind.

A animal

B ird

C ow

D og

E lephent

F inch

G oat

H og

I gwana

J agwier

K angaroo

L epord

M ole

N orwale

O strege

P arrot

Q uail

R at

S nail

T urrtle

U nicorn fish

V ulture

W hale

X erus

Y ak

Z ebra

Scientists used a **ROBOT** **disguised** as a **penguin** to study real emperor penguins.

If you could create a robot to do one thing, what would it do? Draw it here.

A **robot** **officiated** a **WEDDING** in Japan.

The first Saturday in February is National Ice Cream for Breakfast Day.

What other foods do you like to have for breakfast? Finish this table setting with your ideal breakfast feast!

steak

A **photo** of a **potato** once **sold for** more than a **million dollars.**

Jelly Bean

Doritos

Banana

eggs

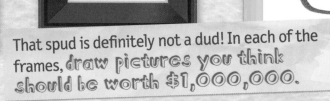

That spud is definitely not a dud! In each of the frames, draw pictures you think should be worth $1,000,000.

In the 1950s, **dyed goat hair** was used for miniature golf **putting greens.**

Start

It's the 18th hole and this golfer is on his way to winning! Help get his ball into the final hole.

A **warm golf ball** will **travel farther** through **the air** than a **cold one.**

18th
Hole

13

The Washington National Cathedral

in Washington, D.C., U.S.A., has a sculpture of **Darth Vader's** head on it.

Darth vader

Draw a few more sculptures of animals, superheroes, or even your favorite movie characters to keep Darth Vader company.

Some DIAMONDS fall to Earth from outer space.

If a dimond feel in my hand

I would make a ring out of it.

16

If a diamond suddenly landed in your hand from outer space, what would you do with it? Write a story about it here.

Scientists found a 99-million-year-old **dinosaur tail** preserved in amber.

Get crazy finishing the drawing of this dinosaur—don't forget the tail!

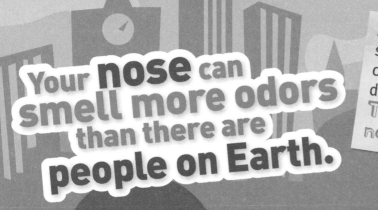

Your nose can smell more odors than there are people on Earth.

A giant nose has taken over the city, sniffing away all of the scent, and nobody can smell anymore! With a friend, use a die to move through the board game. The winner defeats the nose and regains their smell!

START

You found some NASAL SPRAY! Move forward 1 space.

You slipped in SNOT! Go back 3 spaces.

You figured out the giant nose is allergic to GNOMES! Move forward 2 spaces.

You found a HANDKERCHIEF! Move forward 1 space.

SNEEZE attack! Go back 3 spaces.

The giant nose sprayed you with PERFUME! Go back 4 spaces.

... I give up!

FINISH

Candy corn
was originally called
Chicken Feed.

Decorate the candy corn to look like chickens and decorate the chickens to look like candy corn.

Nailympia is a **competition** in which people **decorate** their **fingernails** with anything from **diamonds** and **pearls** to **dolls** and **action figures.**

Wow!

Give these nails some crazy, competitive style.

Your **nails** grow slower in the **winter** than in the **summer.**

Your **fingernails** grow at least **two times faster** than your **toenails.**

One ASTRONAUT took DIRT from the PITCHER'S MOUND at Yankee Stadium into SPACE.

What would you take into space? Draw everything you'd pack in your suitcase!

Slime
glue
water

In **Pennsylvania, U.S.A.,** it is **illegal** for a **fortune-teller** to **tell** someone **where to dig** for **treasure.**

Finish drawing this mystical treasure map, and don't forget to draw the treasure to be found at the end.

Crocodiles sometimes climb trees.

Decorate this crocodile's tree house. Does it need a tire swing? A hammock?

23

According to one study,
surgeons who play **video games**
make **37 percent** fewer mistakes.

start

You've fallen into a surgical video game and this patient needs your help! Make your way through the body to each of the weird items that shouldn't be there. Once you have found each item, finish your procedure by finding the final path out of the body.

1

2

3

8

end

PAINTING
was once an
OLYMPIC SPORT.

What would you like to make an Olympic sport? Draw the competition here.

One rare plant grows only on top of diamond deposits.

That might just be the fanciest plant in the whole world! What do you think a garden made from diamond deposits should look like? Maybe flowers have petals made of jewels, or crowns fit for kings and queens grow on bushes. Create your own sparkling, shimmering garden here!

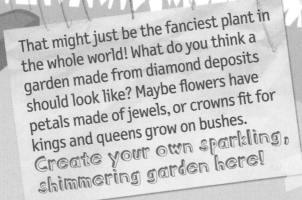

26

A Chinese warrior is said to have stunned enemy troops into retreat by juggling nine balls at once.

Special talents …

I want to learn …

What are some of your unique, special talents? What are a few things you'd like to learn how to do? List them here.

One designer made **a fancy headpiece** out of **crushed soda cans**.

You can buy your **cat a hat** with **bunny ears** on it.

```
A N W O R C P Y P L T
E E R R K I O A L T A
B I Z C R B C A R V B
A N H A W L B L I E A
R A T O L E T A R E R
E E C U S K T E H I O
K B K A O O T S S S D
L S B T R B Y C O O E
A I D S A E S M L E F
T F B E K H B D T B Y
S E A C R R W A R B A
R Z O Z E B H A L A I
S B E J R R C P Y I R V Z O A
E E E I O Z O P R S Y T E I R
A K D E J T D T D A O B S B W
```

Hats off to you if you can find all the hilarious headgear vocabulary in this word search! Words may be found horizontally, vertically, or diagonally, and forward or backward.

AVIATOR
BASEBALL
BEANIE
BERET
COWBOY
CROWN
DEERSTALKER
DERBY
FEDORA
FEZ
JOCKEY'S
PIRATE
SKULLCAP
SOMBRERO
STRAW HAT
TOP HAT
TRILBY
WIZARD'S

400 years ago, English women **decorated** their **hats** with **carrot leaves.**

Octopuses have blue blood.

Octopuses can SEE with their skin.

End

An octopus has nine brains.

Start

This octopus is trying to make its way through the reef. Can you help it get back to its cozy den in the rocks?

Laika the dog was the first astronaut to travel into space.

Mix and match the words from each column above to make exciting dog astronaut names; then color in the dogs inspired by some of your favorite new space dog names!

Example: **Turbo Time-Traveling Tail-Wagger**

Fluffy
Furry
Soft
Cuddly
Stinky
Fuzzy
Drooly
Four-Legged
Turbo
Sniffing
Floppy-Eared
Flea-Ridden
Scruffy
Bearded

Galactic
High-Flying
Turbo
Rocket
Time-Traveling
Alien
Android
Blasting
Space

Fido
Puppy
Dog
Fur Ball
Moon-Hugger
Stargazer
Astronaut-Licker
Space-Drooler
Tail-Wagger
Good Boy
Cowboy
Pawstronomer
Invader

You can buy insurance that covers alien abductions.

If aliens exist, what would you like to say to them? Write your intergalactic space letter here.

Some 20 billion planets in our galaxy could support alien life.

The melody of "Happy Birthday to You" was **WRITTEN** by **two sisters** from Kentucky, U.S.A.

GREEKS started the **tradition** of lighting **candles** on birthdays.

September 16 is the **most common BIRTHDAY,** according to one study.

Decorate this giant birthday cake! Get inspired by your favorite things and your favorite cake flavor, and don't forget those crazy candles.

33

A **picture** painted by a retired **racehorse SOLD** for more than **$2,000** online.

Connect the dots
to find out what the
racehorse is painting.

Candy Bar

Jelly Beans

Ice-Cream Sundae

Cotton Candy

Listening to **high-pitched music notes** makes **food taste sweeter.**

Color in these foods as if they tasted like the sweet food listed underneath them.

You lose up to **100 hairs** a **day.**

Design a few new awesome hairstyles you've never seen before.

There is a **museum** that contains **wreaths** made of **hair.**

Some people use **coffee grounds** to make their **hair shiny.**

A MOUSE can fit through A HOLE the SIZE of a PENCIL ERASER.

This mouse was told that if he could get through this tiny hole, he'd find a crazy, fun, magical land on the other side. **Draw that land here!**

Ready to eat your veggies? Tuck in to this leafy word search. Words may be found horizontally, vertically, or diagonally, and forward or backward.

```
A R E T N A L P G G E C P H S
Z R C B R O C C O L I O O U N
U G R E E N O N I O N R G W C
C C N R O C Y B A B S A A S R
C A U L I F L O W E R T W W R
H L A R T S B C R A E E M E U
I A R P B T A A P R E U B E T
N B U O A I D S C T C M M T A
I R G R R I A H P I U P O P B
R E U E S A E O S C Y E O E A
A S L H G S T P U H E A R P G
E E A L T A A C U O C U H P A
C T E N T C P D A K G C S E A
W T U O R P S S L E S S U R B
U T H L T O H T E A U M M A E
```

ARUGULA
ASPARAGUS
BABY CORN
BROCCOLI
BRUSSELS SPROUT
CALABRESE
CAPSICUM
CAULIFLOWER
CELERIAC
CUCUMBER

EGGPLANT
GLOBE ARTICHOKE
GREEN ONION
HORSERADISH
MUSHROOM
RUTABAGA
SWEET PEPPER
SWEET POTATO
WATER CHESTNUT
ZUCCHINI

Radishes were used to **embalm the dead** in ancient Egypt.

A Canadian slushy company
PRANKS PEOPLE with
GROSS SLUSHY NAMES
but delicious flavors:

SHAVING CREAM = CREAMY ORANGE

PIZZAGHETTI = STRAWBERRY AND KIWI
(PIZZA AND SPAGHETTI)

SOAP = WATERMELON

Dragon fruit

Dream up your own prank slushies. On the cup labels, write the prank name and then what flavor it really is. Then color each slushy cup inspired by your prank flavors.

Dog lovers can satisfy their **craze** for **canines** at a **dog-shaped hotel** called the **Dog Bark Park Inn** in Idaho, U.S.A.

In California, U.S.A., you can **book a room** in an **old school bus.**

STOP

BUS NO. 99

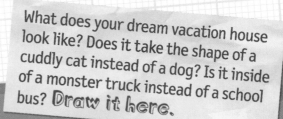

What does your dream vacation house look like? Does it take the shape of a cuddly cat instead of a dog? Is it inside of a monster truck instead of a school bus? **Draw it here.**

December 7 is National **Cotton Candy** Day.

Before 1920, cotton candy was called **"fairy floss."**

Cotton candy was **invented** by a **dentist** in 1897.

What's a fair without cotton candy? Finish the drawing and color this exciting day at the fair!

Pac-Man was inspired by a pizza pie with a slice removed.

Design and draw a video game character based on these food favorites! Then create whatever character your gaming heart desires in the last box.

CUCUMBERS were known as COWCUMBERS until the mid-19th century.

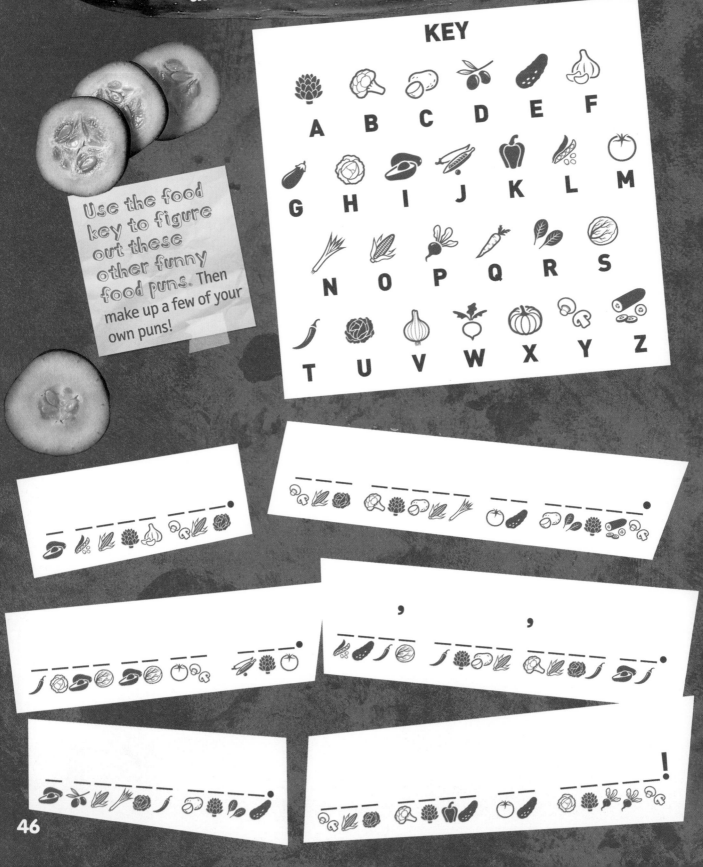

KEY

A B C D E F
G H I J K L M
N O P Q R S
T U V W X Y Z

Use the food key to figure out these other funny food puns. Then make up a few of your own puns!

The world is huge! Can you
countries noted at the
of the page into the g

ACROSS

1 Island with the capital city of Havana
2 Second largest country in the world
6 Chihuahuas are native to this country;
   also a North American country whose
   national language is Spanish
8 This country is the home of the Eiffel Tower
9 The largest city in this country is Madrid
11 Largest country in South America
13 Largest country in the world
14 This Asian country's capital is Seoul
16 The home of St. Patrick's Day
17 Country that Einstein was born in
18 Home of the ancient warriors known as samurai

DOWN

1 This country has more people than any other
3 The capital of this South American country
   is Buenos Aires
4 The home of the kangaroo and koala
5 Hebrew is an official language of this country
7 Country with 50 states
10 Country famous for pizza and pasta
12 South American country that crosses the
    Equator, and whose name means "Equator"
    in Spanish
15 Asian country with the second highest number of
    people in the world

RUSSIA

There is a variety of lemon called a baboon.

Give each of these fruits a new name inspired by an animal.

The first whales had legs.

Draw legs on all of these animals. You can even give some of them shoes!

There is a mountain called **BIG ROCK CANDY MOUNTAIN** in Utah, U.S.A.

With a yummy name like that, *decorate this mountain* with what you think it should have on it!

A **band** once sent a piece of **pizza** into **SPACE** as part of a **music video.**

A **pizza company** once **delivered PIZZA** to **astronauts** in **space.**

What would an alien pizza look like? Would it drive a flying saucer or be topped with something out of this world? Draw the wackiest pie you can imagine here.

In chessboxing,
six rounds of
CHESS
alternate with
five rounds of
BOXING.

Create your own chess figures.
They can have a theme, like your favorite superheroes, or each one can be totally random. Then draw your two favorite pieces duking it out in a boxing match!

Researchers have developed 3-D glasses for insects.

If insects were watching a 3-D action movie, what would it be about and what would the title be? Draw it on the movie screen.

Bonus activity!
Can't get enough of incredible insects? With a parent's permission, check out tons of amazing info, videos, quizzes, and more at *natgeokids.com/insects*.

Finish

One out of every 10,000 clovers is a four-leaf clover.

Start

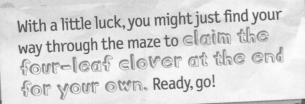

With a little luck, you might just find your way through the maze to claim the four-leaf clover at the end for your own. Ready, go!

Color each of these creatures the wackiest colors you can think of!

The Indian
giant squirrel
has purple fur.

A man once blew a bubble-gum bubble that was larger than a basketball.

These people are having a bubble-gum-blowing contest. **Draw different bubble shapes** coming out of each person's mouth.

The first
bubble gum,
made in 1906,
was called
Blibber-Blubber.

Buttered bread topped with
SPRINKLES
is a popular breakfast
in the Netherlands.

Connect the sprinkles to
see what tasty treat is on the page!

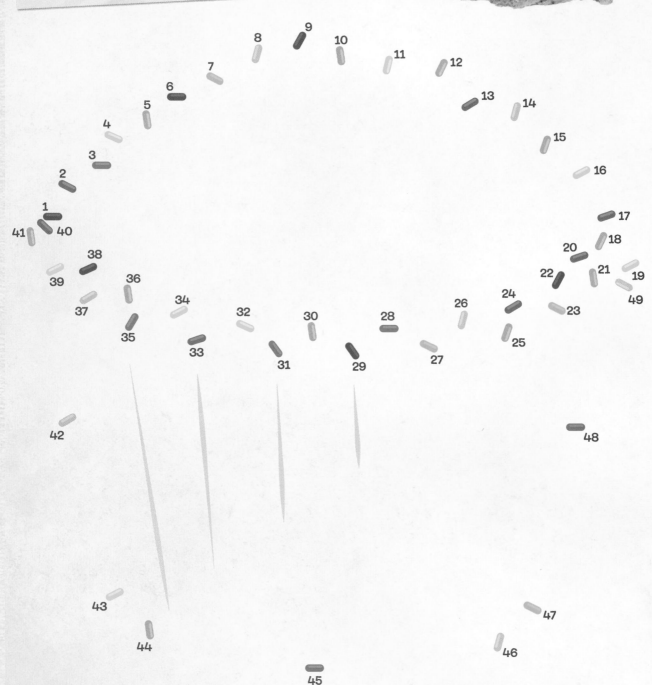

Certain **sharks** walk on their fins underwater.

These walking sharks started their own circus! *Add a shark walking on the high wire, jumping through the hoop of fire, and a shark ringmaster standing on his pedestal.*

In ancient Greece, **comets** were called **"hairy stars."**

What if comets really did grow hair? Give each of these comets a wacky hairstyle!

Dragon-boat racers can row the length of 4.5 football fields in just two minutes.

And they're off! Add wild and colorful dragon features to each of these racing boats.

Humans and dogs perform together in a sport called **musical canine freestyle.**

U.S. president John Quincy Adams had a **pet alligator.**

Our pets are amazing, whether fuzzy, scaly, slithery—or wearing a wig or freestyling! Write a story about your own awesome pet (or a dream pet) and the wacky adventures they might have while you're not home.

Some pet owners pay up to $60 for cat wigs.

A fire started by scientists more than 40 years ago is still burning in Turkmenistan.

Well, if it's still burning, you might as well get some use out of those flames! Add some marshmallows, hot dogs, or your favorite foods to these sticks.

How do you like to eat s'mores? With peanut butter cups instead of plain chocolate, or two chocolate chip cookies instead of graham crackers? Come up with your own crazy s'more creations here.

Some **rainbows** appear to contain only shades of **red.**

What do you think is at the end of a fogbow? Draw it! Then fill in the white rainbow with the craziest colors and patterns you can dream up.

moonbow = a **nighttime** rainbow

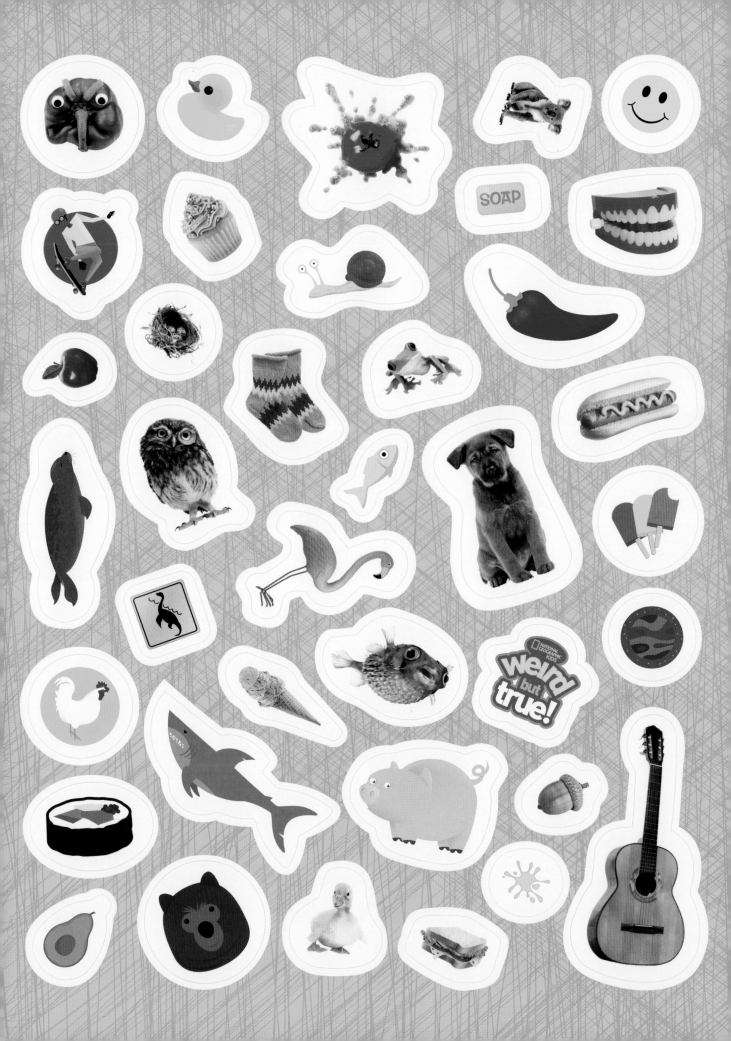

A **fogbow,** also called a **white** or **ghost rainbow,** has a rainbow's familiar arc but no **color.**

Some butterflies' ears are on their wings.

These butterfly bodies need wings, but they don't want just any wings—they want wacky wings! Dream up the wildest wings you can think of.

Butterflies live on every **continent except** Antarctica.

Some
butterflies
drink
turtle tears.

Some **worms** that live on coral reefs **look like** tiny colorful **Christmas trees.**

What a cheerful bunch of worms! Join in on the festivities by decorating this coral reef with Christmas trees and other Christmas decorations.

There is a
DOUBLE-DECKER CAROUSEL
at an amusement park
in CALIFORNIA, U.S.A.

Design your own carousel.
What would humans ride on your carousel? It can be anything from piggybacking on robots to saddling up a polar bear.

The
NATIONAL ZOO
in Washington,
D.C., U.S.A., has a
**SOLAR-POWERED
CAROUSEL.**

At **NEW YORK CITY'S
BRONX ZOO**, you can
ride a **CAROUSEL**
on **GIANT INSECTS**
instead of **HORSES.**

In Connecticut, U.S.A., **a pickle cannot legally be considered a pickle** unless it **bounces.**

Finish

SOAP

Start

Now that's some serious pickle business! Help this bouncy, briny pickle find its fellow pickles in the grocery story.

70

Dogs see only yellow, blue, and gray.

See the world through a dog's eyes by coloring this dog park using only yellow, blue, and gray!

You become
temporarily
paralyzed while
you dream.

You forget most
of your dreams.

Some people dream only in black and white.

You've entered an epic dream world! In each of the floating dream bubbles, draw a scene from one of your favorite dreams, or something you'd like to dream about. Remember, in a dream anything is possible, so don't hold back those wild, wacky, and whimsical thoughts!

There are five times as many bicycles as cars in Copenhagen, Denmark.

START

END

Take a ride through the maze to help the bicyclist find the way home.

Food fight! Color the food splatters to make this food fight come alive. Add some other foods flying through the air.

The annual **Tomato Throwing Festival** in Spain holds the record for the **world's largest food fight.**

At nearly **an inch long, the** (2.5 cm) **pygmy seahorse** can fit into the **palm** of a baby's hand.

The smallest **mammal** ever—a **prehistoric rodent** — was as **big** as your **fingernail** and **weighed no more than** a **dollar bill.**

From teeny tiny to big and bold, animals are amazing. Can you find the rest of the creature cuties in this adorable word search? Words may be found horizontally, vertically, or diagonally, and forward or backward.

```
A F
G W L
E S U O M I         G R
  N P G G E R A A
L G O U M A O L G
G R A A P T B O G
F N S T D M N I B
A M A L L E N T O O T E M
B E F A E I E M A U N S A U
A L L I R O G E T H R K I G
O O L I S B F R L I P T E B
W E I A H E F E   E E B E L Y
L O R E S A A     V M B L E
N P E R R E F     A A A E
A P O I R A S       E C R
H G R B M             B A
```

BEAR	FROG	LION	RABBIT
BEAVER	GIRAFFE	LLAMA	SHEEP
BISON	GORILLA	MONKEY	TIGER
CAMEL	HORSE	MOUSE	TURTLE
ELEPHANT	IGUANA	PRAIRIE DOG	WOLF

76

T. rex's ARMS
were so short, it couldn't scratch its nose!

What else do you think a T. rex's arms were too short to do? Draw it here.

A state fair in Texas, U.S.A., once sold deep-fried soda.

Unscramble the words to figure out what other items have been deep-fried at fairs.

TICKET

BBBEUL MGU
Bubble gum

YELJL NEBSA

LCSEKIP

TICKET

Bacteria talk to each other.

What do bacteria talk about? Fill in the speech bubbles with a funny conversation that only bacteria might have.

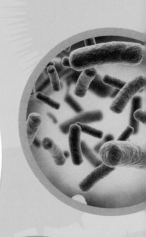
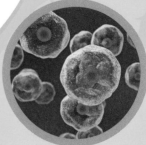

EEHCESKECA

LOKO-IDA

NYADC RABS

ROOES

LSSAA

Australian scientists made swimsuits for sea turtles.

Cannonball! Jump on in and draw funny swimsuits on each of these animals, too.

The average **life span** of an **NBA basketball** is about **10,000 BOUNCES.**

Some early **baseballs** were made of **FISH EYES** covered in **leather.**

Make up your own sports ball and draw it in action!

When designing your sports ball, think of things like:
- What does the court, field, or course look like?
- What is the goal of the game? Is it a team sport or one-on-one?
- Are there any other objects necessary to play the sport?
- What is the name of the ball and the sport?

A shipping container full of
29,000 RUBBER DUCKS
and fellow bath toys FELL OVERBOARD, and
they have since been FOUND all over the WORLD—
in HAWAII, U.S.A.; AUSTRALIA;
and even in THE ARCTIC!

Accessorize these rubber ducks with some fancy and funny outfits that match all of the exciting places they've been.

An **eagle's nest** can stretch wider than your sofa.

Create a cozy living room for this eagle and its sofa-wide nest. Add a TV, chairs, games, or even food!

The world's **biggest flower**— found in the Indonesian rain forest— **can grow wider than a car tire.**

Flower petals can be converted into a diamond.

Find the flowers ready to bloom in this garden word search.

Words may be found horizontally, vertically, or diagonally, and forward or backward.

O R L A C U O A R G S O N T L
U F N C O L U M B I N E O A G
E O A N S U N F L O W E R L M
I R I D R L G L N L S E Y U D
A E L A Z A Y O N U W H M N R
I E O C O R N F L O W E R A A
E C N D A W A O L D H A E P D
H A G M A O I F A T E P G M A
A R A H N D L N N G T N E A F
O N M H A L D A N E H A R C F
R A B L A E S A E O L E B O O
C T G W L Y R W W A L N E A D
H I L I R D S A I S E E R F I
I O O H Y B E G O N I A A M L
D N C H L L L A A E N G H F M

AMARYLLIS
AZALEA
BEGONIA
CAMPANULA
CARNATION
CHRYSANTHEMUM
COLUMBINE
CORNFLOWER
DAFFODIL
DANDELION
FREESIA
GERBERA
GLADIOLUS
GOLDENROD
HYDRANGEA
MAGNOLIA
ORCHID
SUNFLOWER
SWEET PEA
WALLFLOWER

Tulip bulbs were once used as a kind of currency in Holland.

Play-Doh was originally used to clean wallpaper.

This wall looks a little too clean! Make this wall a mess before the Play-Doh cleaning crew arrives.

Gummy bears were originally called dancing bears.

Connect the dots to see what fancy dance these gummy bears are doing!

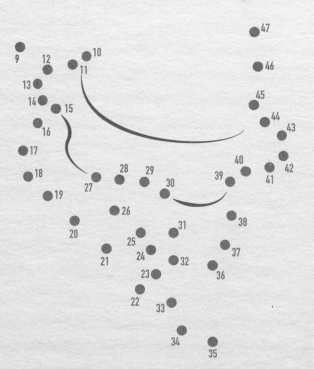

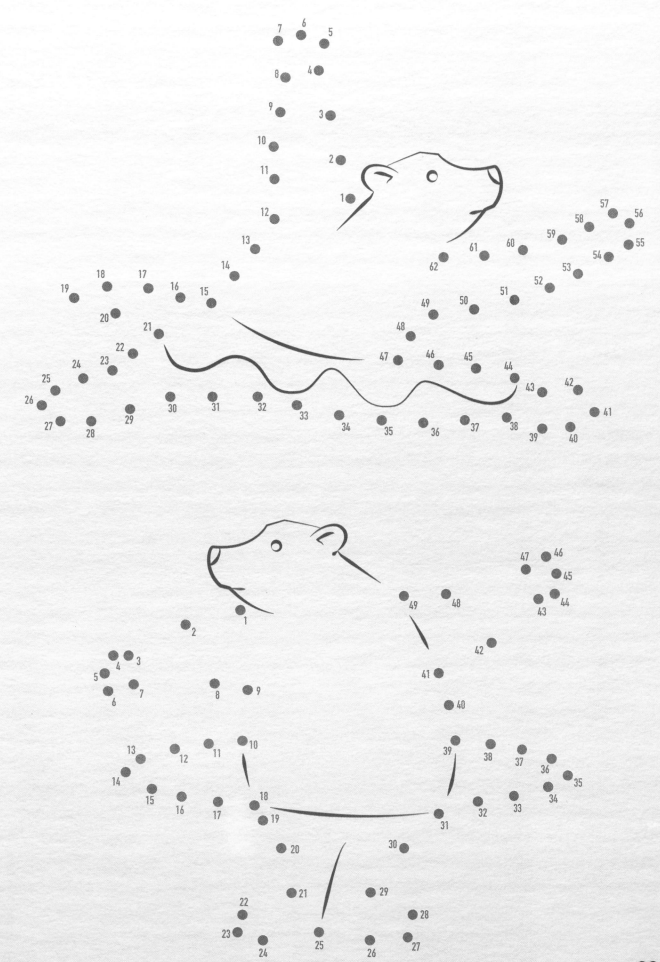

A group of musicians in China makes instruments out of sweet potatoes, carrots, and other vegetables.

Turn your favorite fruits into musical instruments— anything from a hollowed-out-pineapple ukulele to a watermelon-inspired drum set.

College students created a piano out of bananas.

If you started a band with all of your fruity instruments, what would the band name be? Dream up a few fun and fruity band names here.

_____
_____
_____
_____
_____
_____
_____
_____
_____

Bonus activity!

Are you a piano? Or maybe a flute? What about a xylophone? With a parent's permission, head to *natgeokids.com/music-pq*, where you can discover what kind of musical instrument you are in a fun personality quiz.

Some scientists think that plants can learn.

If you could teach a plant to do anything, what would you teach it to do? Clean your room? Sing your favorite songs? Speak a different language? Make a list here. (You could draw it, too!)

This cat is having a splendid spa day. Can you find the seven differences between the two images?

Some pet spas serve catnip tea to feline guests.

Those are some amazing animal powers! A platypus would make one goofy superhero, and an eel or a frog might be its kooky sidekick. Draw a superhero costume on each of them and then give them special superhero names!

Electric eels can use jolts of electricity to control the muscle movements of the fish they hunt.

With their bills, **platypuses** can feel the **electric fields** put out by other animals.

One type of frog **hears through** its **mouth.**

More people have traveled to the **moon** than to the deepest part of the **ocean.**

All right, astronauts—it's time to test your space savvy! Can you fit all the solar system terms at the bottom of the page into the grid?

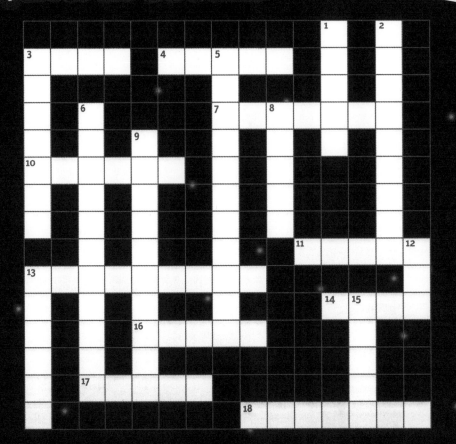

ACROSS

3 The red planet

4 Icy object that leaves a visible trail

7 The farthest planet from the sun

10 The only planet to orbit the sun on its side

11 Largest object in the asteroid belt

13 Space "weather" blowing outward from the sun

14 Planetary satellite

16 Our planet

17 Largest moon of Saturn

18 The largest planet

DOWN

1 Moonless planet, between Earth and the sun

2 Man-made object orbiting the Earth

3 Closest planet to the sun

5 Class that includes asteroids and dwarf planets

6 Class of objects that Pluto belongs to

8 It was once thought to be a planet, but is now considered a dwarf planet

9 The area of the solar system beyond the known planets; also an anagram of "bulkier pet"

12 The center of the solar system

13 Planet famous for its ring system

15 To rotate around the sun

MOON

Bonus activity!
Grab an adult and go to *spaceplace.nasa.gov/menu/play* to make your way through exciting space games, complete with explorer missions, comets, space volcanoes, and much more!

In Madagascar, the **aye-aye** is considered an **omen** of **bad luck.**

Yikes! Counteract all that bad luck with an awesome good-luck charm of your own creation. Draw it here.

Bouquets in Austria have an **odd number of flowers** because some people think **even numbers** are **bad luck.**

According to Cornish **superstition,** it is **bad luck** to **buy a broom** in **May.**

Workers at a shop in California, U.S.A., churn **ice cream** using **bicycles**.

A restaurant in China uses **robots** to cook and serve **meals**.

Some restaurants serve food in **bowls** shaped like **toilets**.

Order up! *Use the menu word search below to find your favorite foods.* Words may be found horizontally, vertically, or diagonally, and forward or backward.

```
L E A C O U S C O U S B Z S O
C U M C H I L L A D A E H A N
K U F A L A F E L B H N D F U
D S A U E R K R A U T R R M F
I N A Y R I B G U C O A A R N
D M O U S S A K A B U C A T L
L E Z T I N H C S R E N E I W
I O S D O R H A A D K O C A C
Y R M U G O G L O F D C L D H
A U S O R R L I U A A I B A O
B H I I O I N R G C N L O O P
M E Z M T E T O D L C I U J S
A O S R A E D E S A O H U I U
M I O O R A D A L I H C N E E
I T A L G E M P A N A D A F Y
```

BABA GANOUSH

BIRYANI

CHILI CON CARNE

CHILLADA

CHOP SUEY

CHORIZO

COUSCOUS

EMPANADA

ENCHILADA

FALAFEL

FEIJOADA

FRANKFURTER

GADO-GADO

IMAM BAYILDI

MACÉDOINE

MOUSSAKA

SAUERKRAUT

SMORGASBORD

TORTILLA

WIENER SCHNITZEL

An
ANNUAL PEA-SHOOTING COMPETITION is held
in the village of
Witcham, U.K.

This punctual pea shooter is supposed to wake up her best friend, but giant peas have rolled into town, blocking different paths! Can you help her find a clear path?

Start

Zzzzzz
Zzzzzz
Zzzzzz

Finish

Before **ALARM CLOCKS**, people
would **SHOOT PEAS** at windows as
a **WAKE-UP** call.

A **Lego** sculpture of **England's Queen Elizabeth II** included a crown with **real diamonds.**

Draw a different sparkling crown on each queen's head. Put a crown on that alien's head, too!

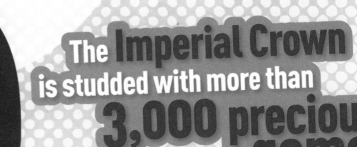

The **Imperial Crown** is studded with more than **3,000 precious gems.**

MENU

Breakfast

Lunch

Dinner

Drinks

Dessert

Dream up your own wacky food combinations for each category on the menu. Think about some of the craziest foods you've ever eaten, or some of your favorite foods that could be combined to make something epically delicious or gross.

Trees with SQUARE TRUNKS grow in PANAMA.

```
        P A T
      O V A L L R I
    S T A R O R E A L
    R E C T A N G L E E R
    E T S E O L E W C S M H H
    I S U L C L R E R D A E P
    K T U D G T E A D I S X Y P C
    T I B I N A L U G C A R E Y E
    L C M A A G O Q E G A N L S E
    N O M I O G S O M T I P R
    C H O R N R N I A N I E C
    R N T R A D G D L H O
    D H A M O E L P N
    O O N R E S E
      L O L
```

Be there or be square: Find more shapes in this totally tubular word search. Words may be found horizontally, vertically, or diagonally, and forward or backward.

There's a huge HEART-SHAPED ICE PATCH on the surface of PLUTO.

CIRCLE	KITE	RHOMBUS
CONE	OCTAGON	SPHERE
CYLINDER	OVAL	SQUARE
DIAMOND	PARALLELOGRAM	STAR
ELLIPSE	PENTAGON	TRIANGLE
HEART	PYRAMID	WEDGE
HEXAGON	RECTANGLE	

Scientists
found a system of
seven Earth-size planets
around a single star
40 light-years away.

The planet
Mercury
is shrinking.

Among the shimmering stars and many moons, can you **find all 10 items that shouldn't be soaring through space?**

A company in England created cheese scented-perfume.

What silly scents would you create if you owned a perfume company? Color and label each perfume bottle.

There is a **store** in California, U.S.A., that only **sells items** inspired by **time travel.**

If you could travel through time, where and when would you go? It can be anywhere in the past or the future, or both! Draw a comic strip of your time-traveling excursion here.

The **Hubble Space Telescope** can **look back** in time.

Water polo players once rode on top of floating barrels painted to look like horses.

Turn these bland barrels into amazing animals.

Peregrine falcons can dive faster than a major league baseball pitcher can throw.

Each of these amazing animals is determined to beat the peregrine falcon in a race, but they might need a little help. Give each one a crazy-cool jet pack or another speedy invention of your own creation!

Some **HOCKEY GAMES** are played on **UNICYCLES.**

The **OLYMPIC TORCH** has been to **SPACE.**

BOWLING dates back to **3200 B.C.**

The world is wild for wacky sports! Can you fit the sports listed at the bottom of the page into the grid?

ACROSS

1. Unarmed combat sport, where the aim is to unbalance an opponent
7. Game that involves knocking down 10 pins
8. A bow and arrow are key requirements for this sport
9. Court-based sport in which the ball is hit with the hand
12. The aim of this sport is to throw the ball through a netted hoop
13. Sport that involves sliding down snowy slopes
14. This sport involves a paddle and a narrow boat
15. You might score an eagle, a birdie, par, or a bogey in this sport
16. An Olympic sport that involves throwing a heavy disk

DOWN

1. You throw a spear in this athletic event
2. If you jump down from a high board into a swimming pool, you're taking part in this sport
3. This sport involves hitting a small puck with hooked sticks
4. This game is an indoor version of a popular outdoor sport played with rackets on a court
5. This sport is like sword-fighting, except with blunt weapons
6. Two teams use their hands to hit a ball back and forth over a net in this sport
8. This is a general term for running, jumping, and other physical sports
10. This sport involves gliding around on wheels or blades
11. In this game you hit a ball back and forth over a net, and possible scores include love and deuce

There's an **app** that lets people rent out their **toilets.**

It's time to get daringly digital and dream up your own phone app. Write about what your amazing app does, and then draw a few of its special features.

Young Roman emperor **Elagabalus** often seated his **dinner guests** on **"whoopee cushions."**

Haven't you always wanted to design your own gag toy? Design your perfect prankster play piece here! Tell everyone what it does, too.

The largest whoopee cushion is **19.78 feet** in diameter—that's longer than an SUV!
(6.03 m)

Early models of the whoopee cushion were called **"boop-boop a doops"** and **"poo-poo cushions."**

What are some other funny names for the whoopee cushion? Make your list here.

Spiders can build webs that are a half mile long.

(0.8 km)

Connect the dots within this spiderweb to see what items the spider has caught.

1
2
3
4
5
8
6
9
7
10
11
12
17
13
16
15
14

42
43
44
45
46
47
48
49
50
24
19
18
20
21
22
23

41
40
39
38
37
36
35
34
33
32
31
30
29
28
27
26
25

113

Earthquakes can instantly create **GOLD** in Earth's crust.

Find the right path through Earth's crust to reach the gold. Watch out for those greedy gophers—they'll do just about anything to get the gold before you do!

START

END

There's an
alarm clock
that **wakes you** up
with **scents**
instead of sound.

What smells are these alarm clocks waking people up with? **Draw a favorite or funny smell in each cloud.**

Can you find all 14 people who are wearing hats made from a corn chip in this picture?

A **corn chip**
shaped like the **pope's hat**
sold for more than
$1,000 online.

Space particles **from** the birth of the **solar system** have been found in building gutters.

Welcome to the final pun-tier: a place where no pun has gone before. Use the decoder to figure out the pun that goes with each picture. Then come up with a few of your own silly space puns!

Just a **teaspoon** of (5 mL) a neutron **star's matter** would weigh **six billion tons.** (5.4 billion t)

KEY

A B C D E F

G H I J K L M

N O P Q R S

T U V W X Y Z

An **astronaut** once lost a **spatula** in space.

A **wrecking ball** was used to let loose **more than 8,000** (3,629 kg) **pounds** of candy held in a **six-story piñata.**

Draw your favorite items flying out of this smashed piñata! It doesn't just have to be candy—get crazy!

A huge arcade in **Laconia, New Hampshire,** U.S.A., features more than **500 video games.**

Design your own arcade room. Along with video game machines, don't forget the prize wall!

Pigs have been taught to play **video games.**

The jack-o'-lantern mushroom glows 24 hours a day and is bright enough to read by at night.

The jack-o'-lantern mushroom is the nightlight for this meadow. Can you finish decorating it? Add some more mushrooms, plants, and anything else you can think of!

420 million
    years ago
mushrooms grew
TALLER
    than giraffes.

A man traveled
from one end of JAPAN
to the other on a scooter.

```
P P C B P A A F P L P F L L T
I R L W L U F I L L O A I E L
L E I A E A L A B O G E P I E
F V F I T F B A T R O D I R R
T I F L K N C P F L S I L E W
N R H C O R L I A E P L F K A
O D A N A A K L O R I S A C L
R B N B N L L F S R N D L I L
F A G T A E U R A A L R L L R
C C E W Y T N E R B F A E C I
L A R O U N D T H E W O R L D
O I O I N W K O O E O B B E E
A P A L R N N O C E E N M E K
R N F R A B A C F L A H U H L
A L E B L E G S W E E P O O K
```

Find your favorite sweet scooter moves in this tricked-out word search. Words may be found horizontally, vertically, or diagonally, and forward or backward.

AIRWALK
ALLEY-OOP
AROUND THE WORLD
BACKFLIP
BANK TRANSFER
BAR CAB
BARREL ROLL

BOARDSLIDE
CABDRIVER
CANNONBALL
CLIFFHANGER
FOOT PLANT
FRONTFLIP
HALF CAB

HEEL CLICKER
LEGSWEEP
POGO SPIN
SCOOTER FLIP
UMBRELLA FLIP
WALL RIDE

The MOST TAILWHIPS
on a scooter
in one minute? 38.

At a WATER PARK in Dubai, United Arab Emirates, riders soar down a 100-FOOT (30-m) SLiDE at 50 MILES AN HOUR. (80 km/h)

Create the ultimate water play day, complete with water balloons, Slip 'N Slides, and whatever else you can think of!

The **world's tiniest guitar** is smaller than a **speck of dust.**

IT IS SMALLER THAN THIS DOT!

Whether teeny tiny or ginormous, see if you can fit all of the musical instruments into the grid.

Across

1 Woodwind instrument with dozens of keys

5 Strummed instrument with six strings

6 Handheld drum that is often played by shaking

10 Largest instrument in the violin family

11 Loud brass instrument, often used for fanfares

14 Double-reeded woodwind instrument

15 Large, bass brass instruments

16 Instrument with lots of wooden bars, each making a different note when hit

17 Bowed instrument that is usually held under the chin to play

Down

1 Clashing percussion instrument

2 Three-sided percussion instrument with a bell-like sound

3 Instrument with lots of strings, played by plucking with the fingers

4 Brass instrument with a slider for playing notes

7 Large, bass woodwind instrument

8 Wind instrument held side-on that you blow across the mouthpiece to play

9 Instrument often associated with jazz

12 Common keyboard instrument

13 Bass violin, held upright on the floor when played

Spider silk has been used to make **violin strings.**

The SPIRITS of OLD UMBRELLAS appear in some JAPANESE MYTHS.

In each box below, *finish designing the mythological creature* that has already been partly created.

Certain **AFRICAN TALES** feature a **SNAKE** that **BELCHES** out **RAINBOWS.**

125

More than **half the world's geysers** are in **Yellowstone National Park** in Wyoming, U.S.A.

Draw yourself doing something exciting outside inspired by an amazing national park.

Nighttime rainbows
are common at
Yosemite National Park
in California, U.S.A.

In late spring, **thousands of fireflies flash in unison** each night for two weeks in Tennessee's **Great Smoky Mountains National Park,** U.S.A.

One **acre of peanut plants** (0.4 ha) can produce **30,000** peanut-butter-and-jelly **sandwiches.**

Come up with your own funky french fry concoctions!

There is a **restaurant** in **Portland, Oregon, U.S.A.,** that serves **peanut-butter-and-jelly fries.**

In **JAPAN,** a chicken restaurant once gave away **PHONE CASES** shaped like **GiANT DRUMSTiCKS.**

Now those are some fiercely fried phone cases! Deck out these phone cases to look just as wacky or way cool.

TWO TEENAGERS IN WISCONSIN, U.S.A., **BUILT A** **ROLLER COASTER** IN THEIR **BACKYARD.**

Draw one wild and wacky thing you wish were in your backyard!

"Watermelon snow" is tinted **pink** and **smells sweet.**

Sounds good enough to eat! Welcome to the world's yummiest snow cone shop. Unscramble the words to figure out the flavor of each snow cone.

Draw your favorite snow cone.

HRITBYAD KAEC

ULEB PEBSRARYR

NNAAAB LPTIS

AINP LDAAOC

NRGAEO AMERC

PPPEIEANL AAABNN

Orange snow once fell in **Siberia.**

130

A crosswalk light in Lisbon, Portugal, features a figure dancing to music as the stop signal.

What dance moves would you like to see the stop signal perform? Fill these boxes with funny or favorite dance moves, like moonwalking or the splits!

High Heel Race =
a race in high heels that sometimes requires heels to be at least
two inches tall
(5 cm)

Draw your own crazy competition!

Gravy Wrestling =
a wrestling match in
264 gallons
(1,000 L)
of gravy

Baby Crawling Race =
babies crawl
12 feet (3.7 m)
to the **finish line**

Roach Racing =
cockroaches are released
in the center of a
20-foot circle
(6-m)
and race to reach the edge first

```
              Y
        M  I  D
     M  L  T  E  R
     U  X  N  I  H  P  S
  M  X  E  S  T  I  G  E  O
  D  O  K  E  Y  R  E  N  O  M  Y
  C  Y  I  A  F  T  E  R  L  I  F  E  S
A  T  A  H  M  D  O  F  O  Y  U  O  X  I  B
D  Y  H  R  O  A  R  E  G  F  E  M  F  R  E
Y  N  I  E  T  A  R  N  L  L  H  I  A  I  B
N  U  I  C  B  O  R  Y  Y  O  S  O  T  S  I
A  U  S  L  A  E  U  A  P  O  L  H  R  O  R
S  V  A  Q  E  S  S  C  H  D  I  R  A  U  C
T  E  S  D  S  U  G  A  H  P  O  C  R  A  S
Y  S  S  O  T  K  S  I  L  E  B  O  K  Y  Y
```

AFTERLIFE

NILE

SARCOPHAGUS

CARTOUCHE

OBELISK

SCRIBE

AMULET

OSIRIS

SPHINX

DYNASTY

PHARAOH

THEBES

EYE OF HORUS

PYRAMID

FLOOD

REEDS

HIEROGLYPH

MUMMY

NEFERTITI

Travel back in time to life in ancient Egypt by completing the word search!

134

There is a town in Colorado, U.S.A., called No Name.

The **50-star American flag** was designed by a **high school student.** His teacher gave him a **B minus.**

Welcome to
_____

A university in **England** has a toilet that **makes ELECTRiCiTY** from pee.

A museum in **Japan** lets kids **slide into a huge toilet** exhibit while **wearing POOP-SHAPED HATS.**

A **toilet-shaped motorbike** in Tokyo uses **fuel made from ANIMAL WASTE.**

Design your own wacky toilets with crazy colors, decorations, and special powers.

Scientists think our **sun** has a **"sibling"**— **a star 110 light-years away** that was born from the same ancient **gas cloud**.

What do you think our sun's sparkling sibling looks like? What if Earth had a sibling, too? Draw the siblings here and then list a few cool and crazy things that might exist on or around them in space!

The original
MR. POTATO HEAD
toy used a
REAL POTATO
instead of a
PLASTIC ONE.

These vegetables want to be famous toys, too. Give them silly faces and accessories.

Help this skateboarder make his way through this crazy skate park full of rad ramps and rails.

Tillman
the English **bulldog**
once skateboarded
328 feet in just
(100 m)
under **20 seconds.**

Kangaroos can **jump** more than **30 feet** (9.1 m) in one hop. That's the length of **12 skateboards!**

The world's biggest **skateboard** is almost as long as a **school bus.**

Finish

141

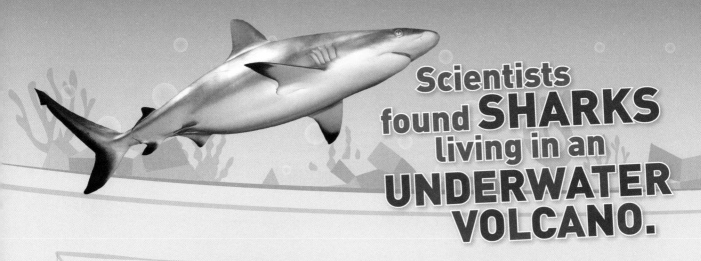

Scientists found **SHARKS** living in an **UNDERWATER VOLCANO.**

Grandma

What would your shark home look like? Finish the drawing with fun shark-fin-inspired furniture or unique underwater decorations.

IN THE FUTURE, you may be able to take a SPACE ELEVATOR thousands of miles above Earth.

Starting from Earth, step into the elevator and **find your way up through Earth's atmosphere** until you've reached the tippy top for an amazing view of space!

END

START

TROPOSPHERE

STRATOSPHERE

MESOSPHERE

THERMOSPHERE

EXOSPHERE

People tend to **SLEEP LESS** when there is a **FULL MOON.**

Can't fall asleep? A full moon is perfect for exploring the forest to see what critters are up to at night. Can you find each animal that is different from its match in this picture? Then color them in.

A man dressed as Santa Claus went skydiving over the North Pole.

Can you find the 14 wacky items in this holiday picture?

acorn	baseball	frog	lightbulb
apple	button	hat	pillow
banana	carrot	hula hoop	pizza
bank		lemon	

Palm trees grew at the North Pole about 55 million years ago.

A RESORT in Fiji will feature an **ALL-GLASS SUiTE 40 feet UNDER THE SEA** (12 m) and access to your own **SUBMARiNE.**

Draw an underwater kingdom that you can explore with your very own supercool submarine.

There's a pedal-powered **roller coaster** at an amusement park in Japan.

There is a **Wizard of Oz–**themed park in Chicago, Illinois, U.S.A.

There's an amusement park in New Jersey, U.S.A., that turns old **construction equipment** into rides.

DIGGERLAND

Welcome to

This amusement park map needs an imaginative genius like you! Fill in any blank signs on the map with ridiculous ride names, and design a few of your own rides, too. Then give your amusement park a neat name and finish off the map with your favorite colors.

ANSWERS

Page 7

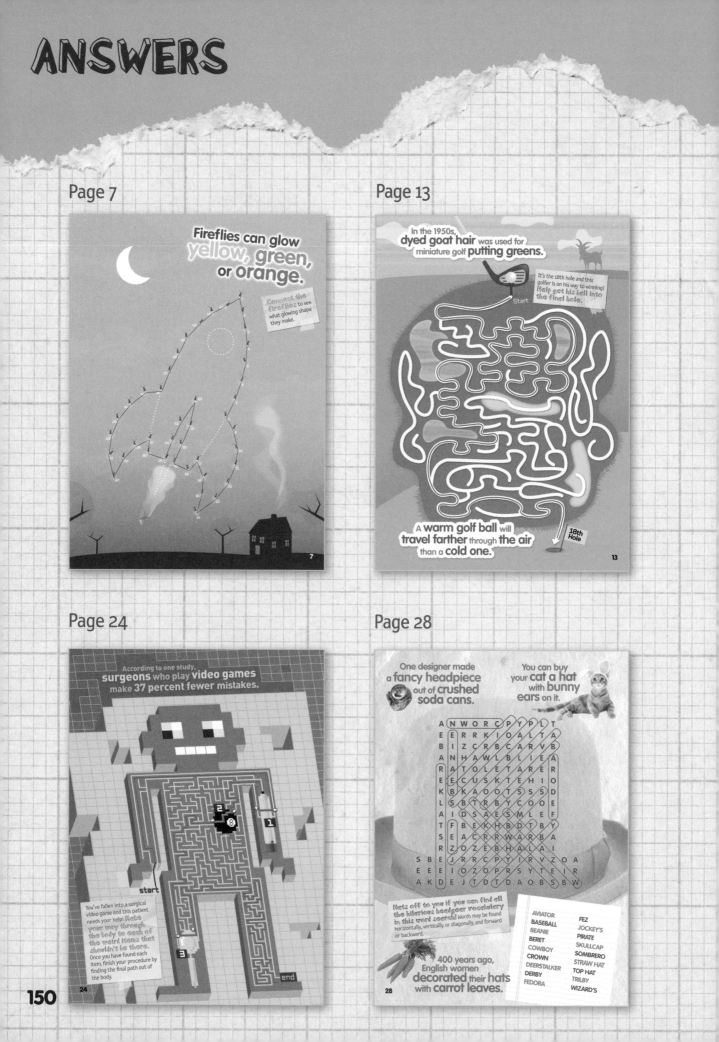

Fireflies can glow **yellow, green, or orange.**

Connect the fireflies to see what glowing shape they make.

7

Page 13

In the 1950s, **dyed goat hair** was used for miniature golf **putting greens.**

It's the 18th hole and this golfer is on his way to winning! Help get his ball into the final hole.

Start

A **warm golf ball** will **travel farther** through **the air** than a **cold one.**

18th Hole

13

Page 24

According to one study, **surgeons** who play **video games** make **37 percent fewer mistakes.**

start

You've fallen into a surgical video game and this patient needs your help! Make your way through the body to each of the weird items that shouldn't be there. Once you have found each item, finish your procedure by finding the final path out of the body.

end

24

Page 28

One designer made **a fancy headpiece** out of **crushed soda cans.**

You can buy your **cat a hat** with **bunny ears** on it.

Hats off to you if you can find all the hilarious headgear vocabulary in this word search! Words may be found horizontally, vertically, or diagonally, and forward or backward.

400 years ago, English women **decorated** their hats with **carrot leaves.**

AVIATOR
BASEBALL
BEANIE
BERET
COWBOY
CROWN
DEERSTALKER
DERBY
FEDORA

FEZ
JOCKEY'S
PIRATE
SKULLCAP
SOMBRERO
STRAW HAT
TOP HAT
TRILBY
WIZARD'S

28

150

ANSWERS

Page 29

Octopuses have **blue blood.**

Octopuses can **see** with their **skin.**

An **octopus** has **nine** brains.

End

Start

This octopus is trying to make its way through the reef. Can you help it get back to its cozy den in the rocks?

29

Page 34

A **picture** painted by a retired **racehorse SOLD** for more than **$2,000** online.

Connect the dots to find out what the racehorse is painting.

34

Page 38

In the 1960s, you could buy celery-flavored Jell-O.

Ready to eat your veggies? Tuck in to this leafy word search. Words may be found horizontally, vertically, or diagonally, and forward or backward.

A	R	E	T	N	A	L	P	G	G	E	C	P	H	S
Z	R	C	B	R	O	C	C	O	L	I	O	O	U	N
U	G	R	E	E	N	O	N	I	O	N	R	G	W	C
L	C	N	R	O	C	Y	B	A	B	S	A	A	S	R
C	A	U	L	I	F	L	O	W	E	R	T	W	W	R
H	L	A	R	T	S	B	C	R	A	E	E	M	E	U
I	A	R	P	B	T	A	A	P	R	E	U	B	E	T
N	B	U	O	A	I	D	S	C	T	C	M	M	T	A
I	R	G	R	R	I	A	H	P	I	U	P	O	A	B
R	E	U	E	S	A	E	O	S	C	Y	E	E	P	A
A	S	L	H	G	S	T	P	U	H	E	A	R	E	G
E	E	A	L	T	A	A	C	U	O	C	U	U	U	A
C	T	E	N	T	C	P	D	A	K	G	C	S	R	B
W	T	U	O	R	P	S	S	L	E	S	S	U	R	B
U	T	H	L	T	O	H	T	E	A	U	M	M	A	E

ARUGULA
ASPARAGUS
BABY CORN
BROCCOLI
BRUSSELS SPROUT
CALABRESE
CAPSICUM
CAULIFLOWER
CELERIAC
CUCUMBER

EGGPLANT
GLOBE ARTICHOKE
GREEN ONION
HORSERADISH
MUSHROOM
RUTABAGA
SWEET PEPPER
SWEET POTATO
WATER CHESTNUT
ZUCCHINI

Radishes were used to **embalm the dead** in ancient Egypt.

38

Page 46

CUCUMBERS were known as **COWCUMBERS** until the mid-19th century.

KEY

A B C D E F
G H I J K L M
N O P Q R S
T U V W X Y Z

Use the food key to figure out these other funny food puns! Then make up a few of your own puns!

I LOAF YOU.

YOU BACON ME CRAZY.

THIS IS MY JAM.

LET'S TACO 'BOUT IT.

I DONUT CARE.

YOU BAKE ME HAPPY!

46

151

ANSWERS

Page 47

AUSTRALIA is WIDER than THE MOON.

The world is huge! Can you fit all the countries noted at the bottom of the page into the grid?

Crossword answers:
CUBA, CANADA, CHINA, ARGENTINA, AUSTRALIA, MEXICO, SPAIN, FRANCE, UNITED STATES, ITALY, BRAZIL, ECUADOR, RUSSIA, SOUTHKOREA, INDIA, IRELAND, GERMANY, JAPAN

ACROSS
1 Island with the capital city of Havana
2 Second largest country in the world
6 Chihuahuas are native to this country; also a North American country whose national language is Spanish
8 This country is the home of the Eiffel Tower
9 The largest city in this country is Madrid
11 Largest country in South America
13 Largest country in the world
14 This Asian country's capital is Seoul
16 The home of St. Patrick's Day
17 Country that Einstein was born in
18 Home of the ancient warriors known as samurai

DOWN
1 This country has more people than any other
3 The capital of this South American country is Buenos Aires
4 The home of the kangaroo and koala
5 Hebrew is an official language of this country
7 Country with 50 states
10 Country famous for pizza and pasta
12 South American country that crosses the Equator, and whose name means "Equator" in Spanish
15 Asian country with the second highest number of people in the world

RUSSIA spans 11 TIME ZONES.

Page 54

One out of every 10,000 clovers is a four-leaf clover.

Finish / Start

With a little luck, you might just find your way through the maze to claim the four-leaf clover at the end for your own. Ready, go!

Page 58

Buttered bread topped with SPRINKLES is a popular breakfast in the Netherlands.

Connect the sprinkles to see what tasty treat is on the page!

Page 70

In Connecticut, U.S.A., a pickle cannot legally be considered a pickle unless it bounces.

Finish / Start / SOAP

Now that's some serious pickle business! Help this bouncy, briny pickle find its fellow pickles in the grocery story.

152

ANSWERS

Page 74

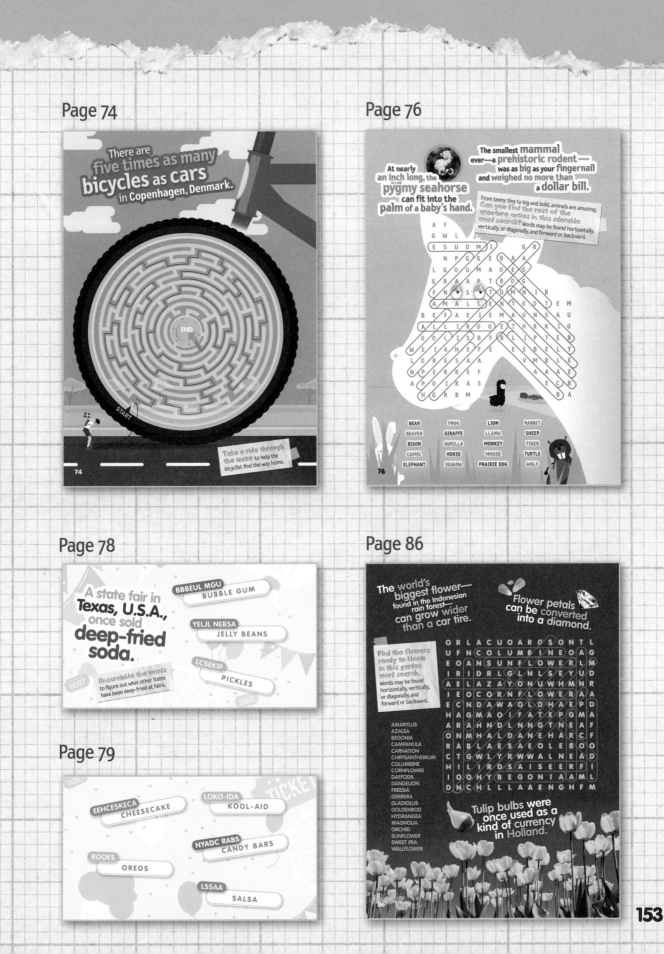

There are **five times as many bicycles as cars** in Copenhagen, Denmark.

END

START

Take a ride through the maze to help the bicyclist find the way home.

74

Page 76

At nearly an inch long, the **pygmy seahorse** can fit into the palm of a baby's hand.

The smallest **mammal** ever—a prehistoric rodent—was as big as your **fingernail** and weighed no more than a **dollar bill**.

From teeny tiny to big and bold, animals are amazing. Can you find the rest of the creature critters in this adorable word search? Words may be found horizontally, vertically, or diagonally, and forward or backward.

BEAR   FROG   LION   RABBIT
BEAVER   GIRAFFE   LLAMA   SHEEP
BISON   GORILLA   MONKEY   TIGER
CAMEL   HORSE   MOUSE   TURTLE
ELEPHANT   IGUANA   PRAIRIE DOG   WOLF

76

Page 78

A state fair in **Texas, U.S.A.,** once sold **deep-fried soda.**

BBBEUL MGU — BUBBLE GUM

YELJL NEBSA — JELLY BEANS

LCSEKIP — PICKLES

Unscramble the words to figure out what other items have been deep-fried at fairs.

Page 79

EEHCESKECA — CHEESECAKE

LOKO-IDA — KOOL-AID

ROOES — OREOS

NYADC RABS — CANDY BARS

LSSAA — SALSA

Page 86

The **world's biggest flower**—found in the Indonesian rain forest—can grow wider than a car tire.

Flower petals can be converted into a **diamond.**

Find the flowers ready to bloom in this garden word search. Words may be found horizontally, vertically, or diagonally, and forward or backward.

AMARYLLIS
AZALEA
BEGONIA
CAMPANULA
CARNATION
CHRYSANTHEMUM
COLUMBINE
CORNFLOWER
DAFFODIL
DANDELION
FREESIA
GERBERA
GLADIOLUS
GOLDENROD
HYDRANGEA
MAGNOLIA
ORCHID
SUNFLOWER
SWEET PEA
WALLFLOWER

Tulip bulbs were once used as a kind of currency in Holland.

86

153

ANSWERS

Pages 88–89

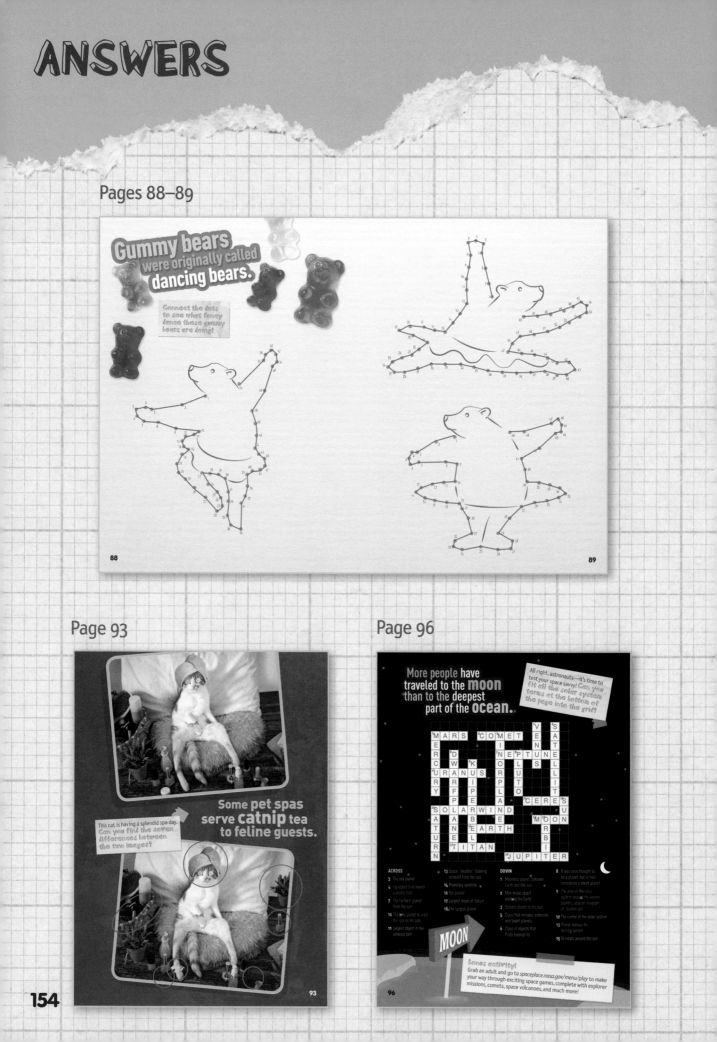

Page 93

Page 96

ANSWERS

Page 98

Workers at a shop in California, U.S.A., churn **ice cream** using **bicycles**.

A restaurant in China uses **robots** to cook and serve meals.

Some restaurants serve food in **bowls** shaped like **toilets**.

Order up! Use the menu word search below to find your favorite foods. Words may be found horizontally, vertically, or diagonally, and forward or backward.

```
L E A C O U S C O U S B Z S O
C U M C H I L L A D A E H A N
K U F A L A F E L B H N D F U
D S A U E R K R A U T R R M F
I N A Y R I B G U C O A A R N
D M O U S S A K A B U C A T L
L E Z T I N H C S R E N E I W
I O S D O R H A A D K O C A C
Y R M U G O G L O F D C L A H
A U S O R R L I U A A I B A O
B H I I O I N R G C N L U D P
M E Z M T E T O D L C I U J S
A O S R A E D E S A O H U I U
M I O O R A D A L I H C N E E
I T A L G E M P A N A D A F Y
```

BABA GANOUSH	CHOP SUEY	FALAFEL
BIRYANI	CHORIZO	FEIJOADA
CHILI CON CARNE	COUSCOUS	FRANKFURTER
	EMPANADA	GADO-GADO
CHILLADA	ENCHILADA	IMAM BAYILDI
		MACÉDOINE
		MOUSSAKA
		SAUERKRAUT
		SMORGASBORD
		TORTILLA
		WIENER SCHNITZEL

98

Page 99

An **ANNUAL PEA-SHOOTING COMPETITION** is held in the village of Witcham, U.K.

This punctual pea shooter is supposed to wake up her best friend, but giant peas have rolled into town, blocking different paths! Can you help her find a clear path?

Start

Finish

Before **ALARM CLOCKS**, people would **SHOOT PEAS** at windows as a **WAKE-UP** call.

99

Page 103

Trees with **SQUARE TRUNKS** grow in **PANAMA**.

ARBOL CUADRADO

Be there or be square. Find more shapes in this totally tubular word search. Words may be found horizontally, vertically, or diagonally, and forward or backward.

There's a huge **HEART-SHAPED ICE PATCH** on the surface of **PLUTO**.

CIRCLE	KITE	RHOMBUS
CONE	OCTAGON	SPHERE
CYLINDER	OVAL	SQUARE
DIAMOND	PARALLELOGRAM	STAR
ELLIPSE	PENTAGON	TRIANGLE
HEART	PYRAMID	WEDGE
HEXAGON	RECTANGLE	

103

Page 104

Scientists found a system of **seven Earth-size planets** around a single star **40 light-years away**.

The planet **Mercury** is shrinking.

Among the shimmering stars and many moons, can you find all 10 items that shouldn't be soaring through space?

104

155

ANSWERS

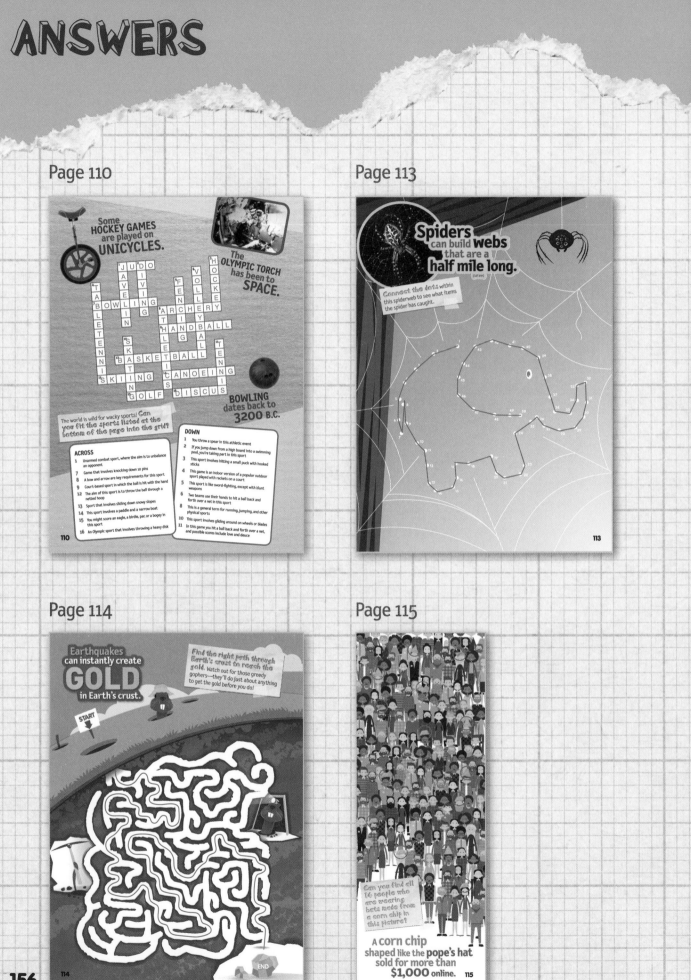

Page 110

Some HOCKEY GAMES are played on UNICYCLES.

The OLYMPIC TORCH has been to SPACE.

```
    J U D O
    A   I
T   V   V       H
A B O W L I N G   O
B   E   N   F   C
L   L   G A R C H E R Y
E   I     T       V   L
T   N   H A N D B A L L
E       L     S       E
N   S   E   B     T   Y
N   K   T   A     E
I   A   I   S K I I N G   N
S   T   C S     K     N
  G O L F   D I S C U S
    N               S
```

BOWLING dates back to 3200 B.C.

The world is wild for wacky sports! Can you fit the sports listed at the bottom of the page into the grid?

ACROSS
1 Unarmed combat sport, where the aim is to unbalance an opponent
7 Game that involves knocking down 10 pins
8 A bow and arrow are key requirements for this sport
9 Court-based sport in which the ball is hit with the hand
12 The aim of this sport is to throw the ball through a netted hoop
13 Sport that involves sliding down snowy slopes
14 This sport involves a paddle and a narrow boat
15 You might score an eagle, a birdie, par, or a bogey in this sport
16 An Olympic sport that involves throwing a heavy disk

DOWN
1 You throw a spear in this athletic event
2 If you jump down from a high board into a swimming pool, you're taking part in this sport
3 This sport involves hitting a small puck with hooked sticks
4 This game is an indoor version of a popular outdoor sport played with rackets on a court
5 This sport is like sword-fighting, except with blunt weapons
6 Two teams use their hands to hit a ball back and forth over a net in this sport
8 This is a general term for running, jumping, and other physical sports
10 This sport involves gliding around on wheels or blades
11 In this game you hit a ball back and forth over a net, and possible scores include love and deuce

110

Page 113

Spiders can build webs that are a half mile long. (full km)

Connect the dots within this spiderweb to see what items the spider has caught.

113

Page 114

Earthquakes can instantly create GOLD in Earth's crust.

Find the right path through Earth's crust to reach the gold. Watch out for those greedy gophers—they'll do just about anything to get the gold before you do!

START

END

114

Page 115

Can you find all 14 people who are wearing hats made from a corn chip in this picture?

A corn chip shaped like the pope's hat sold for more than $1,000 online.

115

156

ANSWERS

Pages 116–117

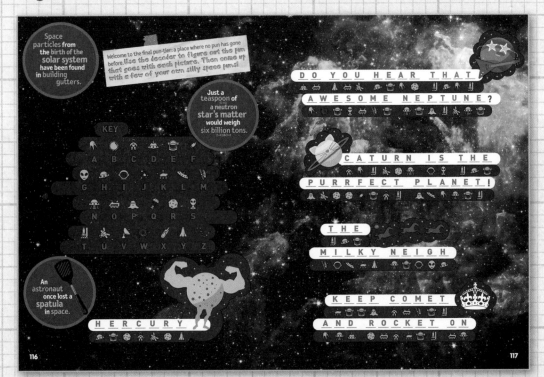

Page 122

Page 124

Find your favorite street scooter moves in this tricked-out word search. Words may be found horizontally, vertically, and forward or backward.

AIRWALK
ALLEY-OOP
AROUND THE WORLD
BACKFLIP
BANK TRANSFER
BAR CAB
BARREL ROLL
BOARDSLIDE
CABDRIVER
CANNONBALL
CLIFFHANGER
FOOT PLANT
FRONTFLIP
HALF CAB
HEEL CLICKER
LEGSWEEP
POGO SPIN
SCOOTER FLIP
UMBRELLA FLIP
WALL RIDE

Across

1 Woodwind instrument with dozens of keys
5 Strummed instrument with six strings
6 Handheld drum that is often played by shaking
10 Largest instrument in the violin family
11 Loud brass instrument, often used for fanfares
14 Double-reeded woodwind instrument
15 Large, bass brass instruments
16 Instrument with lots of wooden bars, each making a different note when hit
17 Bowed instrument that is usually held under the chin to play

Down

1 Clashing percussion instrument
2 Three-sided percussion instrument with a bell-like sound
3 Instrument with lots of strings, played by plucking with the fingers
4 Brass instrument with a slider for playing notes
7 Large, bass woodwind instrument
8 Wind instrument held side-on that you blow across the mouthpiece to play
9 Instrument often associated with jazz
12 Common keyboard instrument
13 Bass violin, held upright on the floor when played

ANSWERS

Page 130

Birthday Cake

Blue Raspberry

Banana Split

Piña Colada

Orange Cream

Pineapple Banana

Page 134

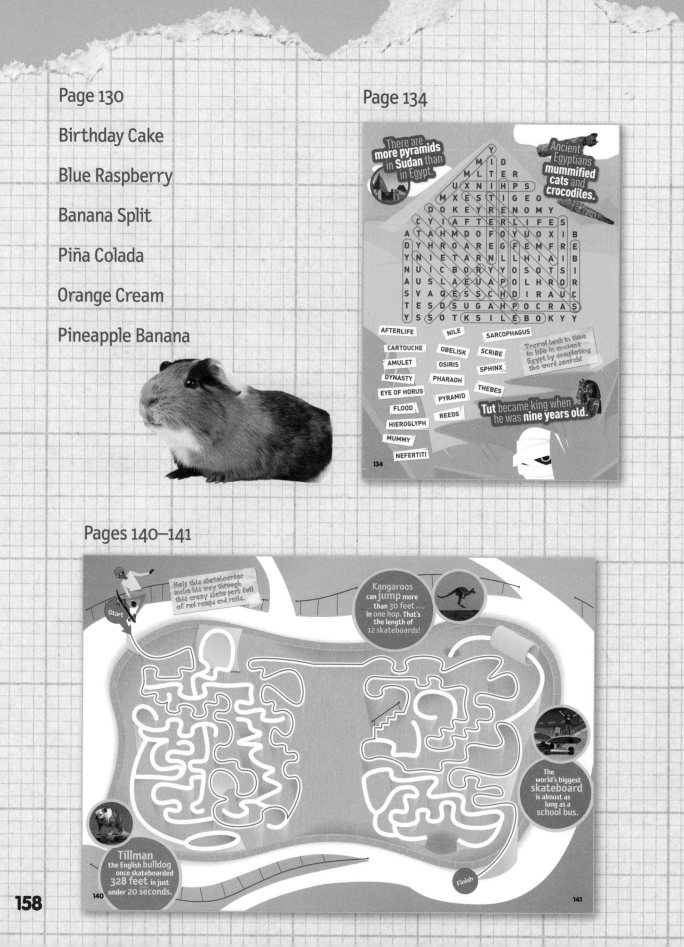

There are **more pyramids** in **Sudan** than in Egypt.

Ancient Egyptians **mummified cats** and **crocodiles**.

AFTERLIFE NILE SARCOPHAGUS

CARTOUCHE OBELISK SCRIBE

AMULET OSIRIS SPHINX

DYNASTY PHARAOH

EYE OF HORUS THEBES

FLOOD PYRAMID

HIEROGLYPH REEDS

MUMMY

NEFERTITI

Travel back in time to life in ancient Egypt by completing the word search!

Tut became king when he was **nine years old**.

Pages 140–141

Help this skateboarder make his way through this crazy skate park full of rad ramps and rails.

Start

Kangaroos can **jump** more than 30 feet in one hop. That's the length of 12 skateboards!

The world's biggest **skateboard** is almost as long as a school bus.

Tillman the English **bulldog** once skateboarded **328 feet** in just under 20 seconds.

Finish

ANSWERS

Pages 144–145

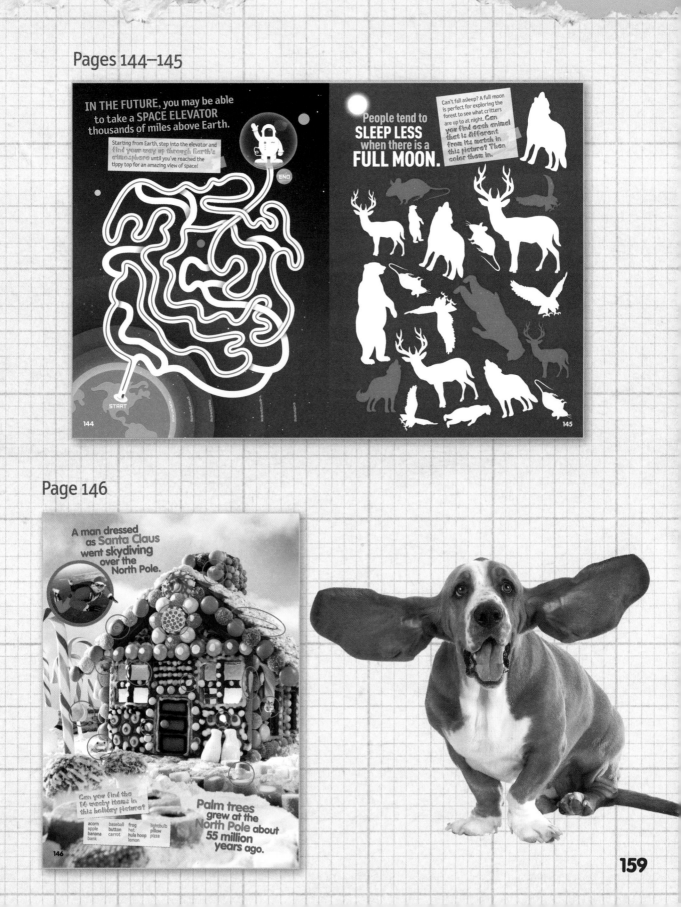

IN THE FUTURE, you may be able to take a **SPACE ELEVATOR** thousands of miles above Earth.

Starting from Earth, step into the elevator and find your way up through Earth's atmosphere until you've reached the tippy top for an amazing view of space!

END

START

144

People tend to **SLEEP LESS** when there is a **FULL MOON.**

Can't fall asleep? A full moon is perfect for exploring the forest to see what critters are up to at night. Can you find each animal that is different from its match in this picture? Then color them in.

145

Page 146

A man dressed as Santa Claus went skydiving over the North Pole.

Can you find the 16 wacky items in this holiday picture?

acorn · baseball · frog · lightbulb
apple · button · hat · pillow
banana · carrot · hula hoop · pizza
bank · · lemon ·

Palm trees grew at the North Pole about 55 million years ago.

146

CREDITS

To Mikey and his lovable laugh. —K.H.

Word searches and crosswords created by Gareth Moore

Illustrations by Kevin McFadin unless otherwise noted

FRONT COVER: (husky), Africa Studio/Shutterstock; (pencil), Boltenkoff/Shutterstock; (gecko), Susan Schmitz/Shutterstock; (hot air balloon), artpritsadee/Shutterstock; (frog with crown), Lightspring/Shutterstock; (yellow dog), SvetPavlova/Shutterstock; (lemur), Eric Isselee/Shutterstock; **SPINE:** (husky), Africa Studio/Shutterstock; (pencil), Boltenkoff/Shutterstock; **BACK COVER:** (pizza), images.etc/Shutterstock; (owl), Isselee/Dreamstime; (koala), Isselee/Dreamstime; (goldfish), Vangert/Shutterstock

INTERIOR: 2 (CTR LE), Carol Buchanan/Dreamstime; 2 (CTR), acarart/iStock; 2 (LO LE), Kuttelvaserova Stuchelova/Shutterstock; 2 (UP LE), itographer/iStock; 2 (CTR LE), Carol Buchanan/Dreamstime; 3 (UP RT), Sean Murphy/Getty Images; 3 (CTR RT), oneo/Shutterstock; 3 (LE), Tony Campbellt/Shutterstock; 3 (LO RT), Viktor1/Shutterstock; 4 (LE), metha1819/Shutterstock; 4 (RT), bogdan ionescu/Shutterstock; 5 (LO LE), Vladyslav Starozh/Shutterstock; 6, Sean Murphy/Getty Images; 8, MattStaples/iStock; 11 (UP LE), Newscom; 11 (LO RT), CB2/ZOB/WENN.com/Newscom; 12 (UP LE), Layland Masuda/Shutterstock; 12 (LO), STILLFX/Shutterstock; 14, Irene Abdou/Alamy; 17, R.C. McKellar, Royal Saskatchewan Museum; 20, CB2/ZOB/WENN.com/Newscom; 25, Picsfive/Shutterstock; 26, oneo/Shutterstock; 28 (UP LE), Hayati Kayhan/Shutterstock; 28 (UP RT), Stephanie_Zieber/Getty Images; 28 (LO LE), Nattika/Shutterstock; 28 (background), Gnilenkov Aleksey/Shutterstock; 29 (UP), Steven Hunt/Getty Images; 30 (UP LE), SPUTNIK/Alamy; 34, Christopher T. Assaf/Baltimore Sun/MCT via Getty Images; 36, Laboko/Shutterstock; 37 (UP), Dave Bredeson/Dreamstown; 37 (UP RT), Maksym Bondarchuk/Shutterstock; 38 (UP), maexico/Shutterstock; 38 (LO), Egor Rodynchenko/Shutterstock; 38 (background), andreasnikolas/Shutterstock; 40, M L Pearson/Alamy; 41, Rich Koele/Shutterstock; 42, Pao Laroid/Shutterstock; 46 (UP), Artville; 46 (CTR), Hein Nouwens/Shutterstock; 47, Aphelleon/Shutterstock; 49, Chris Brown/Alamy; 52, sampics/Contributor/Getty Images; 55 (UP), Robin Chittenden/FLPA/Minden Pictures; 58 (UP), anyamuse/Shutterstock; 58 (CTR), mayakova/Shutterstock; 62, Vice Books/Caters News; 64 (CTR LE), Christian Heeb/Getty Images; 64 (LO), isarescheewin/Shutterstock; 65, Frank Olsen, Norway/Getty Images; 66 (UP), Butterfly Hunter/Shutterstock; 66 (CTR), Butterfly Hunter/Shutterstock; 66 (LO), Kirsanov Valeriy/Shutterstock; 67 (UP), Kesu/Shutterstock; 67 (LO), Kesu/Shutterstock; 68, Kagii Yasuaki/Nature Production/Minden Pictures; 69 (UP), Chuck Eckert/Alamy; 69 (LO), Peter Bennett Ambient Photos/Newscom; 70, Africa Studio/Shutterstock; 71, Odua Images/Shutterstock; 72, Hung Chung Chih/Shutterstock; 73, Hung Chung Chih/Shutterstock; 75, David Ramos/Getty Images; 76, littlesam/Shutterstock; 77, metha1819/Shutterstock; 78 (LE), Peeradach Rattanakoses/Shutterstock; 78 (UP RT), Jezper/Shutterstock; 78 (LO RT), Timbrk/Dreamstime; 79 (UP), Irochka/Dreamstime; 79 (LO), Christian Darkin/Shutterstock; 80, Nick Holmes/Caters News; 85, Paul Nicklen/National Geographic Creative; 86 (UP CTR), Brand X; 86 (UP RT), oneo/Shutterstock; 86 (CTR), TierneyMJ/Shutterstock; 86 (LO), Sailorr/Shutterstock; 87, timquo/Shutterstock; 88, Viktor1/Shutterstock; 90 (LO), Maks Narodenko/Shutterstock; 93, Irina Kozorog/Shutterstock; 94, Hans Leijnse/NiS/Minden Pictures; 95, Roland Seitre/Minden Pictures; 97 (UP), Thorsten Negro/Getty Images; 97 (LO LE), Luchi_a/Shutterstock; 97 (LO RT), Straw broomstick/Shutterstock; 98 (UP RT), Sipa Asia/REX/Shutterstock; 98 (UP LE), Quirky China News/REX/Shutterstock; 100, Adrian Dennis/Getty Images; 103 (UP LE), Buiten-Beeld/Alamy; 103 (LO RT), NASA/APL/SwRI; 105, Edward Westmacott/Shutterstock; 106 (LO RT), Nerthuz/Shutterstock; 106 (background), Anatolii Vasilev/Shutterstock; 108 (UP), Steven Oehlenschlager/Dreamstime; 108-109, IDEAPIXEL/Shutterstock; 110 (UP LE), Peter Downs/Getty Images; 110 (UP RT), Yuri Kochetkov/Epa/REX/Shutterstock; 110 (LO RT), terekhov igor/Shutterstock; 111, Milkovasa/Shutterstock; 113, papkin/Shutterstock; 115, Hong Vo/Shutterstock; 115 (RT), ProStockStudio/Shutterstock; 116-117, LynxVector/Shutterstock; 116 (LO LE), Artville; 120 (UP), Darlyne A. Murawski/National Geographic Creative; 120 (LO), George Grall/National Geographic Creative; 122, ffolas/Shutterstock; 124 (UP), Photo by D. Carr and H. Craighead, Cornell; 124 (LO), Szasz-Fabian Jozsef/Shutterstock; 125, AVS-Images/Shutterstock; 126, Robynrg/Shutterstock; 127 (UP), Don Smith/Getty Images; 127 (LO), Floris van Breugel/Nature Picture Library/Alamy; 128 (UP), Hong Vo/Shutterstock; 128 (LO), Potato Champion; 129, Courtesy YUMI Brands; 132 (UP LE), EPA/Mark R. Cristino/Newscom; 132 (LO), Alan Martin/Contributor; 133 (UP), Kazuhiro Nogi/Staff/Getty Images; 133 (LO), Bradley Kanaris/Stringer/Getty Images; 134 (UP LE), urosr/Shutterstock; 134 (CTR RT), Gianni Dagli Orti/REX/Shutterstock; 134 (UP RT), Greg Watts/REX/Shutterstock; 134 (LO RT), Jaroslav Moravcik/Shutterstock; 136, The Asahi Shimbun/Contributor/Getty Images; 137, Yoshikazu Tsuno/Staff/Getty Images; 140, Doug Meszler/Splash News/Newscom; 141 (UP), Janelle Lugge/Shutterstock; 141 (CTR RT), Solent News/Splash News/Newscom; 142, Carol Buchanan/Dreamstime; 145, ntnt/Shutterstock; 146 (background), PaulMichaelHughes/Getty Images; 146 (UP LE), Graiki/Getty Images; 146 (CTR), Bryan Solomon/Shutterstock; 146 (LE), Maks Narodenko/Shutterstock; 146 (LO LE), halimqd/Shutterstock; 146 (UP LE), mama_mia/Shutterstock; 146 (UP CTR), images.etc/Shutterstock; 146 (CTR RT), annt/Shutterstock; 146 (UP), Dionisvera/Shutterstock; 146 (UP), Dionisvera/Shutterstock; 146 (UP RT), StanislauV/Shutterstock; 146 (CTR), cocoo/Shutterstock; 146 (UP CTR LE), Marques/Shutterstock; 146 (CTR RT), jannoon028/Shutterstock; 146 (CTR), Palokha Tetiana/Shutterstock; 147, REX/Shutterstock; 148 (UP), Buddhika Weerasinghe/Stringer/Getty Images; 148 (LO), Richard Ellis/Alamy; 149, Richard Ellis/Alamy; 158, MattStaples/iStock; 159, WilleeCole Photography/Shutterstock

All sticker art by Fan Works Desgn unless otherwise noted. **STICKER PAGE 1:** (green pepper with face), Carl Stewart/Shutterstock; (smashed tomato), Okea/Getty Images; (koala), Isselee/Dreamstime; (cupcake), Ruth Black/Dreamstime; (mouth), Hurst Photo/Shutterstock; (apple), rimglow/iStock; (nest), optimarc/Shutterstock;

(socks), alex_kz/iStock; (frog), Sascha Burkard/iStock; (hot dog), Valentina Razumova/Dreamstime; (owl), Isselee/Dreamstime; (dog), Africa Studio/Shutterstock; (Loch Ness monster sign), Jeff Morin/Shutterstock; (flamingo), Eivaisla/Shutterstock; (ice cream), Designsstock/Dreamstime; (pufferfish), Eric Isselee/Shutterstock; (acorn), Dionisvera/Shutterstock; (guitar), unclepepin/Shutterstock; (duckling), Levente Gyori/Dreamstime; (sandwich), Loopall/Dreamstime; **STICKER PAGE 2:** (hot air balloon), tulpahn/Shutterstock; (Easter egg), Hannamariah/Shutterstock; (praying mantis), Ziva_K/Getty Images; (hands, both), samara_p/Shutterstock; (ice pops), graja/Shutterstock; (rubber duck), photodisc; (peacock), Hintau Aliaksei/Shutterstock; (goldfish), Vangert/Shutterstock; (plane), ConstantinosZ/Shutterstock; (money), urfin/Shutterstock; (mug), urfin/Shutterstock; (rabbit), djem/Shutterstock; (bird), FocusDzign/Shutterstock; (clock photo), stockshoppe/Shutterstock; (pinwheel), Hurst Photo/Shutterstock; (doughnut), Bryan Solomon/Shutterstock; (rocket), Early Spring/Shutterstock; (potatoes), Anneka/Shutterstock; (squash with glasses), Carl Stewart/Shutterstock; **STICKER PAGE 3:** (box of chocolates), Photastic/Shutterstock; (purple button), Picsfive/Shutterstock; (skunk), Ultrashock/Shutterstock; (spring), tialhuni/Shutterstock; (puffin), Eric Isselée/Shutterstock; (whoopee cushion), Luca Montevecchi/Shutterstock; (cookie), stockphoto-graf/Shutterstock; (mailbox), TRINACRIA PHOTO/Shutterstock; (ghost), rangizzz/Shutterstock; (bald eagle), Eric Isselée/Shutterstock; (blue robot), HomeStudio/Shutterstock; (alien sign), Jeff Morin/Shutterstock; (black chicken), Aksenova Natalya/Shutterstock; (phone), prapass/Shutterstock; (duck), Vasyl Helevachuk/Dreamstime; (Chihuahua), Africa Studio/Shutterstock; (eggs), Luis Louro/Shutterstock; **STIKCER PAGE 4:** (robot), HomeStudio/Shutterstock; (kittens), absolutimages/Shutterstock; (film), AlinaMD/Shutterstock; (penny), rsooll/Shutterstock; (mask), Dimedrol68/Shutterstock; (camera), Sashkin/Shutterstock; (lightbulb), Somchai Som/Shutterstock; (pink button), Picsfive/Shutterstock; (Bigfoot), Jeff Morin/Shutterstock

Since 1888, the National Geographic Society has funded more than 12,000 research, exploration, and preservation projects around the world. The Society receives funds from National Geographic Partners, LLC, funded in part by your purchase. A portion of the proceeds from this book supports this vital work. To learn more, visit natgeo.com/info.

NATIONAL GEOGRAPHIC and Yellow Border Design are trademarks of the National Geographic Society, used under license.

For more information, visit nationalgeographic.com, call 1-800-647-5463, or write to the following address:
National Geographic Partners
1145 17th Street N.W.
Washington, D.C. 20036-4688 U.S.A.

Visit us online at nationalgeographic.com/books

For librarians and teachers: ngchildrensbooks.org

More for kids from National Geographic: natgeokids.com

For information about special discounts for bulk purchases, please contact National Geographic Books Special Sales: specialsales@natgeo.com

For rights or permissions inquiries, please contact National Geographic Books Subsidiary Rights: bookrights@natgeo.com

Designed by Fan Works Design, LLC

The publisher would like to thank the following people for making this book possible: Kate Hale, senior editor; Julide Dengel, art director; Christina Ascani, associate photo editor; Paige Towler, associate editor; Alix Inchausti, production editor; Sally Abbey, managing editor; and Anne LeongSon and Gus Tello, production assistants.

Trade paperback ISBN: 978-1-4263-3023-0

Printed in China
18/IHKFLC/1

BYE!